The Joint Military Intelligence College supports and encourages research on intelligence issues that distills lessons and improves support to policy-level and operational consumers

This series of Discussion Papers will present the work of faculty, students, and others whose research on intelligence issues is supported or otherwise encouraged by the Joint Military Intelligence College through its Office of Applied Research. Discussion Papers are used in instruction and research activities of the College, and undergo prepublication review by College Faculty.

Proposed manuscripts for these papers are submitted for consideration to the Applied Research Editorial Board. Manuscripts or requests for additional copies of Discussion Papers should be addressed to Defense Intelligence Agency, Joint Military Intelligence College, Center for Strategic Intelligence Research, MC-X, Bolling AFB, Washington, D.C. 20340-5100.

Russell.Swenson@dia.mil, **Editor**

Discussion Paper Number Twelve

EXPERIENCES TO GO: TEACHING WITH INTELLIGENCE CASE STUDIES

By Thomas W. Shreeve, Col (USMCR)

JOINT MILITARY INTELLIGENCE COLLEGE
WASHINGTON, DC
September 2004

CONTENTS

Foreword v

Introduction 1

Case Research and Casewriting 2

How to Write an Effective Teaching Note 6

Evacuating the Americans from Rwanda Case Study 8

Teaching Note for Use with Rwanda Case Study 18

The Bombing of the Marine Barracks in Beirut Case Study 22

The Bombing of the Marine Barracks in Beirut: The Long Commission
  Report 38

Teaching Note for Use with Lebanon Case Study 42

About the Author 47

EXPERIENCES TO GO: TEACHING WITH INTELLIGENCE CASE STUDIES

FOREWORD

Colonel Thomas W. Shreeve, USMCR, is a former faculty member of the Master's Program for Reserves at the Joint Military Intelligence College. For several years, Colonel Shreeve, in CIA's Office of Training and Education, developed and refined the case-study method of teaching intelligence principles and procedures. His cases, including some used at Harvard University's John F. Kennedy School of Government, are realistic and historically accurate. The validity of intelligence case studies presupposes the existence of academic theory or, alternatively, worldly practice that constitutes "theory-in-action." The National Foreign Intelligence Community, of course, offers a quintessential example of the latter, making the case studies described here both valid and reliable for a variety of instructional environments. Colonel Shreeve's advice and examples for writing a teaching note can guide a novice case-method instructor toward an effective classroom analysis of cases.

Readers should recognize that a good deal of difference exists between the teaching-oriented case studies in this paper, on the one hand, and research papers using the case study design wherein sources are explicitly identified, the event context more fully explored, and the research questions carefully related to a theoretical superstructure through pertinent conclusions. Case studies generate important questions for student consideration, using the broad range of evidence derived from empirical observations by respective authors and other contributors to each case.

Comments pertaining to this paper are invited and should be forwarded to: Director, Center for Strategic Intelligence Research, Joint Military Intelligence College, DIAC, Bolling AFB, Washington, DC 20340-5100.

Dr. Russell G. Swenson, Director, Center for Strategic Intelligence Research

EXPERIENCES TO GO: TEACHING WITH INTELLIGENCE CASE STUDIES

INTRODUCTION

Long associated with teaching at the graduate level in business and public administration, the case method represents a structured approach to learning from the past. The method relies on the use of historically accurate, written descriptions of events or dilemmas that students read, analyze, and meet to discuss under the guidance of an instructor. Instructors use questions to guide the discussion toward a particular pedagogical destination rather than declarative statements that tell students how or what to think about a complex issue. Learning by the case method is active rather than passive, as students are explicitly made partners in the reduction of ambiguity surrounding complex, realistic issues.

Students who learn by the case method improve their analytic skills when instructors ask them to identify the problems at hand and they fortify their decisionmaking skills when instructors ask them to propose a plan of action to resolve the problems they have identified. Driven by the constructive conflict that typically results from a group's examination of a complex issue, case-based discussions frequently also result in improved student ability to express individual convictions in the face of criticism from peers.

Any description that provokes thoughtful reflection and is historically accurate may be considered for use in a case-based class. The term "case" refers to a description of a dilemma that stops short of the outcome. The term "case study" refers to a description of a past event that has an outcome included in the document and thus is known to the students. Both vehicles are equally useful; case studies tend to be longer, more detailed, and more historical in tone.

The use of case studies as a basis for teaching in the intelligence profession requires a body of well-crafted cases and case studies that are relevant to the needs of students and faculty. There are a number of prospective sources for such material. External sources include civilian academic institutions such as the John F. Kennedy School of Government at Harvard. The JFK School's catalog includes several dozen cases and case studies that may be appropriate for classroom use. This is particularly true for courses that feature the relationship between intelligence and national security policy; about a dozen JFK School cases examine this relationship in detail. Most of this material was created under a contract between the JFK School and the Central Intelligence Agency (CIA)'s Center for the Study of Intelligence. JFK School cases and case studies explore strategic issues, whereas CIA material addresses the tactical or operational levels of war, where many if not most JMIC graduates will spend their intelligence careers.

Another external source is the Intelligence Community Case Method Program, which has about 200 cases and case studies, many of which may also be appropriate for classroom use. Almost all of these are classified and cover a wide variety of dilemmas and events drawn directly from the experience of personnel from CIA, the State Department, the Armed Forces, and other elements of the U.S. Intelligence Community. Several of the case studies focus exclusively on military intelligence and counterintelligence issues, chiefly at the tactical and operational levels of war.

Other sources offer long-term value as they can be tailored specifically for classroom needs. One possibility is to convert selected existing master's theses into case studies by careful editing and revision. The theses are available immediately and at no cost; however, a considerable investment of time and effort is required to convert them to the form of a case study. Another internal source is through faculty and student research and publication. Research by students supervised by faculty is probably the best long-term source of prospective cases and case studies.

Instructors who are unfamiliar with the case method or who need to refine their skills may benefit from attending an instructor workshop on the technique. Two workshops are conducted by Harvard University faculty, one in Cambridge meeting one afternoon per week for nine weeks and the other conducted sporadically at conferences of the American Society for Training and Development. The third is the CIA's three-and-a-half day Case Method Teaching Workshop (CMTW), which can be conducted onsite.[1]

Advantages of the CMTW include its low cost and the speed with which it can be used to familiarize a sizable number of interested instructors; it is also tailored specifically to the U.S. Intelligence Community. More than 250 Community instructors, including several from the Armed Forces, have attended the CMTW. Special iterations have been conducted for the U.S. Naval War College, the Armed Forces Staff College, the Marine Corps Command and Staff College, and the Navy and Marine Corps Intelligence Training Center. Experience at several military educational institutions suggests that the use of cases and case studies can result in successful, engaging discussions.

CASE RESEARCH AND CASEWRITING

Teaching by the case method requires a supply of relevant, well-crafted cases and case studies. These are a unique literary form: part history, part drama, part research paper.

Fitting the Case Into a Course

The first requirement for a successful case is to understand how it will fit into a specific course. The instructor *and* the casewriter (these may be the same person) must know what teaching points are to be communicated to the students by their exploration of the case. In courses in which several cases will be used, instructors need to examine carefully how the concepts that students will derive from each one will fit together, so that the students can apply what they have learned to new and increasingly difficult material.

---

[1] For further information on the Case Method Teaching Workshop, contact Tom Shreeve at (703) 237-4624 or at *tomshreeve@aol.com*, and visit the website at *http://www.intelcasestudies.com*.

Finding the Right Context

Once an instructor/casewriter has a clear idea of the teaching points, he or she needs to find a situation that will serve as an appropriate context for the case or case study. Fortunately, the diverse and often intrinsically exciting operations of the Central Intelligence Agency make this part of the task fairly easy. Sources for good leads include colleagues in various parts of the organization, former students, and sometimes specific Agency components. For example, the Office of Personnel, Special Activities Staff, is an excellent source for cases dealing with "problem employees," while the Office of the General Counsel or the Inspector General Staff are natural places to look for cases involving legal or ethical conflict.

Recruiting Sources

Once on the trail of a potential case, the instructor/casewriter needs to contact the people who were involved in it and persuade them to cooperate. This is not always easy, especially in cases in which people have made mistakes—something we all do but which we don't especially want untold numbers of future students to examine in exhaustive detail! The process of persuading the sources of a case to reveal what happened is, I suspect, a little like recruiting sources of foreign intelligence. The sources—especially the main characters in the drama—must *trust* the casewriter, or they will not be candid. Earning that trust requires absolute fidelity, in my experience, to a few simple rules:

- Never reveal to anyone else what a source has told you without the source's permission. Moreover, you must be sure that the more substantial sources of your case see your drafts before the material is used in the classroom, and that they have the opportunity to change material that is inaccurate, offensive, or embarrassing. If you don't do this, you will not succeed as a casewriter—it's as simple as that.

- Don't quote one source to another. Frequently sources in a case will not entirely agree about events and their meaning. This is normal, because we often tend to see things differently, but encouraging conflict among sources by highlighting disagreement diminishes your chances of using your case in class.

- Listen carefully to what is said *and* to what is not said. It is fair to challenge sources to provoke them to be more specific or more forthcoming, but do it with courtesy and respect. You are not trying to prove anything with your case—you are just telling a story from which people can learn to make better judgments and decisions.

Research

While recruiting the sources and winning their trust, the instructor/casewriter should gather background material about the situation that will help him or her understand what is going on. Often, written material is available that will provide useful insights into the history and culture of the organization in which the action occurs, and some of this will be helpful to students, too. Other times there is only anecdotal evidence, which is better than nothing.

For cases that are particularly difficult or which present students with challenging quantitative data, it may be necessary to include a good deal of background material to orient readers to the dilemma under study. This is particularly true of *case studies*, which are typically richer in historical detail than *cases*. Where appropriate, one can place quantitative and some other types of material in "exhibits" at the end of a basic document.

Writing and Editing the Case

Good cases require room for disagreement among equally well-informed and intelligent readers as to what the main characters should do in the dilemma described. Indeed, *constructive conflict* is the engine that drives this method of teaching. The reader should have all the basic data that the protagonist had when the need for decision or action arose; but if it is obvious what the protagonist should do, the discussion is not likely to be very productive.

Write the case in a story-telling style. Students can more readily identify with the characters in the case if the characters have personal names and some descriptive data— if they can be accepted as real people. Further, students can identify better with the main decisionmaker in the case if they have something in common with that character, such as age, experience, type of assignment, and so on. This isn't absolutely necessary, and sometimes it doesn't matter at all, but it's something to keep in mind, especially for an audience that is very narrowly focused.

Cases should be clear and concise. This does *NOT* mean that the dilemma described in the case should be unambiguous (indeed, requiring students to untangle ambiguity is part of the point to this method), but that the students should have no difficulty understanding what was ambiguous about the problem, and why. It is very helpful to have other people, including colleagues, supervisors, or editors review your material. Also, most case method teachers like to "pilot" a new case with colleagues before trying it in the classroom. This is a good way to identify gaps and errors, and to get an idea of the classroom dynamics that the case is likely to create.

Getting the Case Released

The casewriter should have cases formally "released" by the sponsoring organization before using them in class. Usually, though not always, this should be done in writing, with a note or a letter from a responsible officer in the sponsoring organization that explicitly allows the use of the case. (This is a separate step from assuring the main sources that they have the right to edit the material.) Sometimes, getting a case released may require that it be moderated or "watered down" in some way. This is unfortunate, but it is better than not using the case at all. Infrequently, the sponsoring organization will get cold feet after the case is completed, and will insist that it be diluted past the point of usefulness. This may test your powers of persuasion, or your patience, or both. No easy answer exists for this problem.

It is almost always possible to disguise the characters in a drama with pseudonyms, and one can, if appropriate, even make up fictitious components in order to get a case released for use in class. The sources and the releasing organization must, of course, be comfortable with any disguises used. In the "user's note" at the bottom of the first page, one may tell the reader what has been done in this light. When characters are so prominent that they cannot possibly be disguised (Rick Ames, for example), there is no reason not to use true names. It is better to use pseudonyms, however, even for people who have resigned or retired, simply out of respect for their privacy.

Credibility

Some OTE cases have been made up, and some of these have been used successfully for years. However, hypothetical cases subvert one of the strongest features of the case method: a grounding in reality. Cases have much greater credibility with students if the students understand that what they are discussing actually happened, and that something very similar could happen personally to them, and soon. Cases can be created which appear as real as those that are *really* real, but at the Central Intelligence Agency, good cases are so plentiful that finding them is easy.

A Final Word

Cases are not meant to illustrate either the effective or the ineffective handling of administrative, operational, logistic, ethical, or other problems, and the characters in cases should not be portrayed either as paragons of virtue or as archvillains. The instructor/casewriter must be careful not to tell the students what to think—they are not empty vessels waiting to be filled with wisdom. With this method of teaching, a major share of the responsibility for thinking critically about the issues under discussion is shifted to the students, where it belongs.

Below is a "casewriter's template" that includes questions casewriters will find helpful as a point of departure when writing an Intelligence Community case or case study. Casewriters do not necessarily need to answer all of the questions on the template, but by at least considering each one, the writer will be more likely to head in the right direction from the beginning.

A Casewriter's Template

Who is the client for this case? What does the client need?

In one sentence, what is the overall purpose of this case?

What are the teaching objectives? (List no more than four, each expressed in not more than three sentences.)

What is the subject-matter knowledge level of the students who will use this case? (The answer to this question will influence the amount of background material included in the case and its level of conceptual difficulty.)

Where does the action in the case occur? Is permission secured from a senior manager in this component to proceed with research and writing?

To what written records will access be needed? Who has custody of these records?

Who must be interviewed? How can they be contacted?

How much time will be required to complete the research and writing phases of this case?

What graphics can be used? (Getting these identified and produced early can save time; these tasks can occur in parallel with research.)

Have those individuals or components who have a substantial stake in the case had an opportunity to review the material that is based on their cooperation or in which they are prominently mentioned? Has permission for quotes attributed to them been secured?

Who will release the case? Does he or she understand its purpose?

HOW TO WRITE AN EFFECTIVE TEACHING NOTE

A teaching note is the map for the intellectual journey that a case-based discussion represents. A strong teaching note significantly increases the probability that an instructor will arrive successfully and on time at the pedagogical objectives of a case or case study. This is particularly true when the instructor is using material that he or she did not personally research and write. Effective teaching notes tend to evolve as instructors acquire experience with a case or case study, and instructors should be prepared to revise their teaching notes substantially in the early stages of the normal lifespan of a case or case study.

Effective teaching notes include a brief summary of the story, the teaching objectives, a suggested teaching plan that includes discussion questions that will move the discussion from one block of analysis to the next, and some guidance concerning the timing of these questions. If appropriate, a teaching note may also include a suggested "board plan," or an outline of what a classroom chalk or marker board should look like in order to lend emphasis and structure to the instructor's summary at the end of the discussion.

A teaching note should begin with a brief summary of the case in one or two paragraphs, highlighting the central issues of the case. A description of the intended classroom context may also be included, with reference to the professional discipline of the audience and the level of experience or skill that may be required before students are able to benefit fully from a detailed discussion of the material. For their academic value, teaching notes may also include a reference to the research techniques that the casewriter employed, and to the details of coordination, if appropriate.

A teaching plan—the most important part of the teaching note—begins with the identification of the objectives. These should be stated briefly, and should be few in number—I suggest no more than four. Instructors should keep these in mind; they are the "destination" of the journey. The objectives are simply those concepts that instructors want students to internalize—the central lessons of the discussion. It is important that the objectives be stated simply, and instructors should not be concerned with getting students to "parrot" the objectives as written in the teaching note.

The teaching plan should then suggest a lead-off question, designed to get students headed in the most productive direction. Strongly recommended as a lead-off question is one that is fairly easy to answer and that requires little analysis. It is helpful to establish the norm of student participation early in the discussion, and a difficult question or one that requires extensive analysis is unlikely to accomplish this goal. A teaching plan should include reference to the range of probable responses that the lead-off question is likely to provoke, so that instructors are well-prepared to keep the discussion on track in its early stages.

The teaching plan should clearly identify the "blocks of analysis" that represent the milestones in the journey. These are the main ideas or concepts that students should visit on their progress toward the objectives. At each milestone, instructors should be prepared with "probing questions," designed to push students to inquire into the issues of the case in greater depth or with increased sophistication as they wrestle with each block. "Bridging questions" are those that are designed to move from one block of analysis to the next as the discussion evolves. It is helpful to include a rough sense of timing, so that instructors have a sense of how much time should be spent in discussion of each block of analysis.

A useful teaching note may also include a board plan, and experience suggests that the best board plans are very general. To the extent possible, instructors should use the board as a general structure for their summary at the end of the discussion, highlighting reflections of teaching and learning objectives as they have emerged from student contributions. Ideally, instructors will refer to individual contributions that moved the discussion in a productive direction to its ultimate intellectual destination. For example, pointing to a student contribution on the board, an instructor might say, "As John observed at the beginning of our discussion, the incentive system in the Directorate of Operations puts a high premium on recruitment at the expense of counterintelligence concerns."

If the case or case study is part of an overall plan to reinforce theoretical concepts provided to students through other pedagogical techniques, a teaching note should suggest ways in which instructors can link the discussion to knowledge, principles, or skills that the students have acquired. A strong teaching note reinforces the central idea of case-based teaching: that the instructor's job is to guide the group toward the objectives through the use of questions rather than declarative statements. When students discover the objectives through their own efforts and articulate them in their own words, the class will have reached the paramount expression of case-based teaching.

EVACUATING THE AMERICANS FROM RWANDA[2]

On Wednesday, 6 April 1994, second-tour Foreign Service Officer Pamela Smith was the State Department Duty Officer for the U.S. Embassy in Kigali, Rwanda. Then 26 years old, Pamela sought the assignment to Kigali because she hoped that in a small Embassy she would acquire experience at a wider range of Department functions and have greater autonomy than as a member of a larger staff. Pamela and her husband Jack arrived in Rwanda in August 1993.

The Embassy staff consisted of seven other officers, including the Ambassador, the Deputy Chief of Mission (DCM), an administrative officer, a General Services Officer (GSO), two communicators, and a secretary. Pamela was the consular officer and also served as the econ/commercial officer and military security assistance officer. The Embassy community also included 10 personnel from the Agency for International Development (AID) and a public affairs specialist from the U.S. Information Service (USIS). There was no Marine Security Guard detachment. The Regional Security Officer (RSO) was based in Bujumbura, Burundi, and visited the post in Kigali periodically. The defense attache—U.S. Army Lt. Col. Mike Kalinowski—visited Kigali three times annually from his post in Yaounde, Cameroon. After his arrival in Kigali, Jack Smith was hired on a local contract as the assistant GSO.

At this time there were 258 Americans in Rwanda, including representatives of private firms, nongovernmental organizations, and missionary groups. Some 60 American children attended the Kigali International School. In April 1994, the admin officer was on leave, and the AID director had recently departed the post. Colonel Kalinowski had just arrived for a one-week visit.

Pamela and the other Americans had grown accustomed to the occasional gunfire that marked the longstanding conflict between Rwanda's two major ethnic groups, the Hutus and the Tutsis. In October 1993, UN forces had arrived to enforce a fragile peace agreement, according to which the Tutsi-dominated Rwandan Patriotic Front (RPF) was allowed to position a 600-man battalion on the grounds of the Rwandan Parliament building. Uprisings had continued in February 1994, with some 200 killed in ethnic violence, prompting Ambassador David Rawson's order to revise and expand the Embassy's emergency action plan. As the junior member of the Emergency Action Committee, which was headed by Deputy Chief of Mission (DCM) Joyce Leader, Pamela was deeply involved in the details of this planning.

---

[2] This case study is based on open sources and on interviews with State Department officers who were directly involved in the events described. The case study was written in February 1995 by CIA instructor Tom Shreeve and Foreign Service Institute instructor Dana Dee Carragher. "Pamela Smith," "Jack Smith," "Mike Kalinowski," "Andrew O'Dwyer," and "Lew Giordano" are pseudonyms. The photographs were taken by Pamela Smith. This, and all cases and case studies may be used with the permission of Tom Shreeve. He is available at (703) 237-4624 or at *tomshreeve@aol.com.*

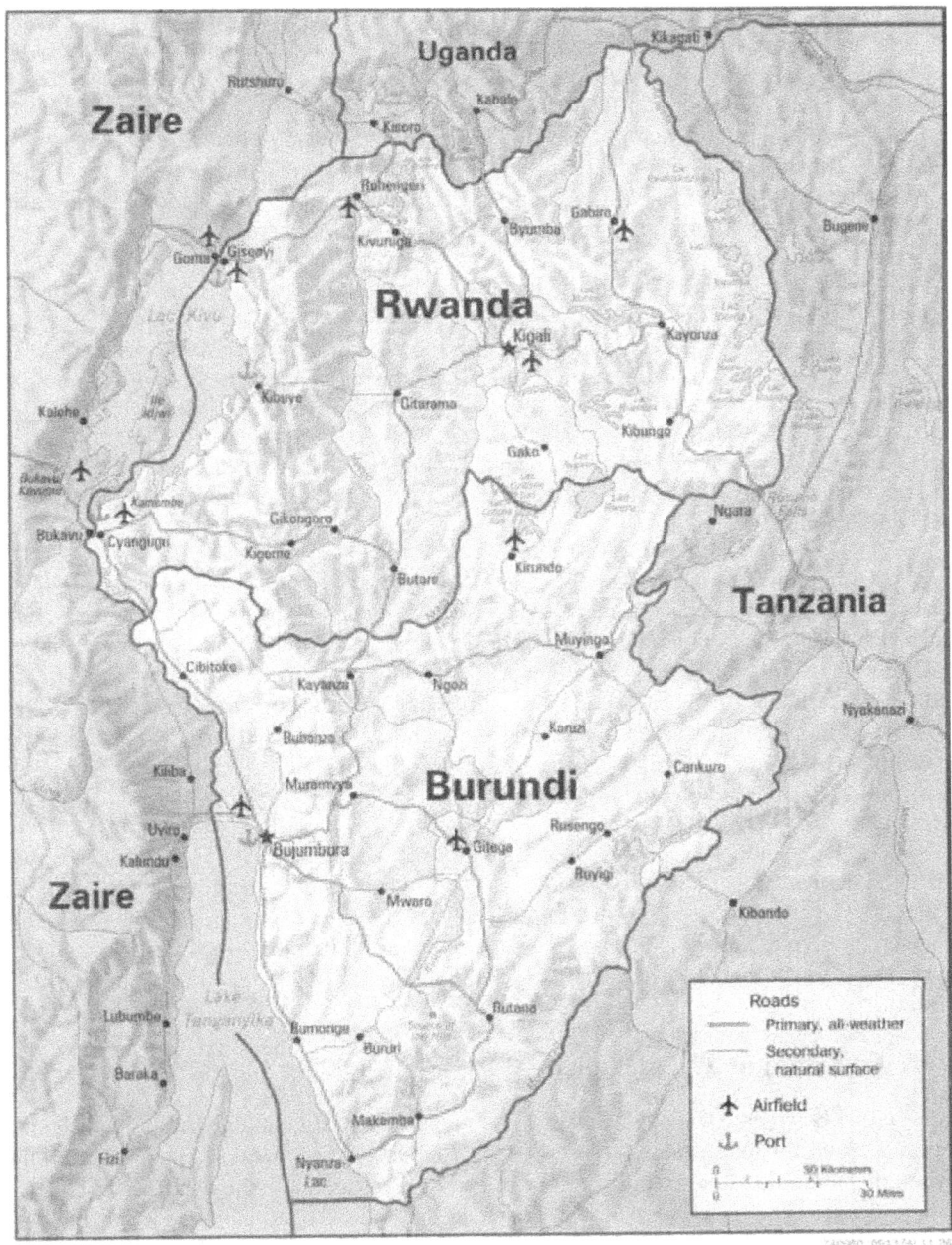

Rwanda and Burundi.

As part of her planning, Pamela made a point of personally meeting every one of the Americans residing in Rwanda, even those in outlying areas. She set up a schedule of regular meetings with all of them, 15 or 20 at a time. She collected information about each individual and kept it in two identical files, one at the Embassy and one in her home. In addition to the name of each person, the files included date and place of birth, passport number and issue date, next-of-kin in the United States, telephone number or radio call-sign, and a list of dependents, if any. For those in remote areas of Rwanda, Pamela also included a photograph of each American citizen.

On that Wednesday evening, Pamela and Jack were joined at dinner in their home by Colonel Kalinowski. Other Americans also were present. At around 2100 hours, Pamela and the others heard a muffled explosion from the direction of the airport, some 12 kilometers away. Jack Smith, who was a former U.S. Marine, looked at Colonel Kalinowski. "Colonel, that didn't sound like a grenade. It was something bigger."

Colonel Kalinowski nodded his agreement. "Let's see what we can find out." Pamela began to call a number of contacts she had developed in the Rwandan military and among UN commanders.

The Americans did not yet know it, but the sound they heard was made by the fiery crash of a French-built aircraft carrying Presidents Juvenal Habyarimana of Rwanda and Cyprien Ntaryamira of neighboring Burundi and eight others returning from Dar es Salaam, Tanzania, where they and other African leaders had met in an attempt to end the ethnic warfare that plagued Rwanda and Burundi. All aboard the aircraft were killed. In a variety of statements soon issued in Kigali and at UN headquarters in New York, Rwandan Government officials claimed the aircraft had been brought down by gunfire or a missile of some kind on its approach to the airport.

The crash of the Presidents' aircraft triggered a nightmare of ethnic violence that resulted in the deaths of hundreds of thousands of Rwandans. Over the next several days, Pamela's duty would be to coordinate the evacuation of the American citizens—most of them members of missionary groups or commercial contractors—residing in Rwanda who faced grave danger. The Emergency Action Committee's planning would now be tested.

A Tradition of Tribal Violence

Conflict between Rwanda's two major ethnic groups, whose members spoke the same language and shared similar religions, had a history dating back to the 15th Century when the nomadic Tutsi moved south from Ethiopia to dominate the agricultural Hutu, a Bantu people. The area that eventually became the nations of Rwanda and Burundi was populated by about 85 percent Hutus and about 14 percent Tutsis. European colonial powers—at first Germany and later Belgium—allied themselves mainly with the dominant Tutsi. Shortly before granting independence to their former colony in Rwanda in 1962, the Belgians turned political, economic, and military power over mainly to the Tutsi. The majority Hutus objected violently and lashed out in a 1959 uprising in which many thousands of Tutsis were killed and another 200,000 fled into neighboring Burundi and Uganda. The two groups had fought each other savagely since then in a cycle of bloody reprisals.

In October 1990, a group of about 2,000 Rwandan exiles belonging to the Rwandan Patriotic Front (RPF) invaded northeastern Rwanda from their bases in Uganda, threatening President Habyarimana's regime and raising the specter of renewed ethnic violence. This group—mainly but not exclusively Tutsi—soon was joined by other Tutsis and disaffected Hutus, bringing the exiles' strength to around 20,000. An RPF-led rebellion dragged on for the next several years. After nearly a year of negotiations, the Hutu-dominated Rwandan Government and the Tutsi-dominated RPF reached a fragile agreement in August 1993, with both sides agreeing to the deployment of UN troops to help ensure peace.

Efforts to form a transitional government acceptable to both groups quickly stalled in an atmosphere of mutual distrust. The two slain presidents had agreed to meet in Dar es Salaam to continue the talks, hoping to avert full-scale civil war in Rwanda. These hopes were dashed by the attack on the returning aircraft as extremists on both sides sought revenge or political advantage. Within a few hours of the crash, members of Habyarimana's Presidential Guard—joined by bands of Hutu extremists known as the Interhamwae, a ragtag militia armed mainly with clubs and machetes and with a well-earned reputation for viciousness—went on a rampage, killing dozens and perhaps hundreds of their opponents, chiefly Tutsis and moderate Hutus.

The Warden System

Within an hour of the attack on the Presidents' aircraft, U.S. Ambassador David Rawson telephoned Joyce Leader to relay the news of the fatal crash. Leader heard similar reports soon after on a Rwandan radio station. Together, Rawson and Leader composed a message to relay to the U.S. community through the "warden system," a network of 15 selected members of the American community, known as wardens, who volunteered to maintain communications between the Embassy and other U.S. citizens during a crisis. The wardens also served as observers, reporting critical information back to the Embassy. Each warden had a specific list of individuals for whom he or she was responsible. As news was passed to the warden, he or she would send it on by telephone, by radio, or in person. If an evacuation were to become necessary, the Ambassador planned to use this system to convey the Embassy's instructions and assemble personnel.

The DCM immediately contacted Pamela Smith, who relayed the Ambassador's message by radio and telephone, telling the members of the American community to hold fast and wait for further word at 0700 the next morning.

Colonel Kalinowski returned to his nearby hotel. Throughout the night, Pamela and Jack could hear the sound of mortars and both light and heavy machinegun fire. A number of wardens called in, reporting that the road to the airport, which ran past the Parliament building where the RPF battalion was headquartered, was under heavy fire.

A Rwandan Army Armored Personnel Carrier (APC) was permanently posted outside the US Embassy during the first few days of fighting between Rwandan factions.

Thursday, 7 April

In his 0700 hours radio message, the Ambassador confirmed the Presidents' deaths and instructed all the Americans to remain inside their homes. Pamela and Jack spent most of Thursday on the telephone, reassuring the Americans—many of them now on the edge of panic—who called in. At around 1045 hours, while on the phone with the DCM, Pamela could hear Rwandan soldiers break into her residence and loudly accuse her of hiding Rwanda's interim Prime Minister Agathe Uwilingiyimana, who lived next to Joyce and had developed a friendship with her. Unable to escape into the DCM's compound, Uwilingiyimana sought refuge in the nearby UN Development Program complex, but was quickly discovered there by Rwandan soldiers and shot to death. Other members of the Rwandan Cabinet and their families also were killed. Also on Thursday morning, a group of 10 Belgian soldiers of the UN peacekeeping force were disarmed and brutally murdered by the rampaging gangs as the city gave way to anarchy.

From her home, Pamela began to call contacts she had developed among Rwandan officials and members of other embassies. Earlier, whenever she had reason to deal with Rwandans on either side of the ethnic conflict, Pamela had made a point of assuring them of her neutrality in the fight between the Tutsi-dominated RPF and the Hutu-dominated Rwandan Government. Now that neutrality began to pay off, as Rwandan military officials stated that the mainly Hutu Rwandan Army would not fire on Americans. They could not, they added, speak for the RPF.

Pamela relayed news of her contacts to the Ambassador, but on Thursday night, the telephone lines to the neighborhood where the Ambassador lived were cut. Further, the Ambassador lived in an area that was directly between the centers of the two warring factions, and there was heavy fighting around his home. It was clear that Rawson was not going to be able to get to the Embassy any time soon. The high-frequency radio he kept at his residence enabled the Ambassador to stay in contact with Nairobi, however, and through that route he could communicate with senior State Department officials in Washington.

Friday, 8 April

Hoping soon to be able to move to the Embassy where they could better carry out the evacuation, Jack had packed camping gear and personal firearms for himself and Pamela. (As a former Marine Security Guard, Jack was skilled with firearms and had encouraged Pamela to practice shooting. They owned two 9 mm pistols, a 12-gauge shotgun, and a hunting rifle.) On Friday morning, Colonel Kalinowski called from his hotel. "I'll be there in five minutes," he said. "Be ready to get in your car immediately and we'll get to the Embassy."

Right on schedule, Colonel Kalinowski showed up with a Rwandan Army escort accompanied by Peace Corps volunteer Andrew O'Dwyer, who happened to be staying in the same hotel as Colonel Kalinowski. Pamela, Jack, Andrew, and Colonel Kalinowski entered the Embassy without incident around 1100 hours on Friday.

Using their contacts among Rwandan Government officials and in the RPF, Colonel Kalinowski and Pamela began negotiating the details of an evacuation of the trapped Americans. In their negotiations, they relied on occasion on a group of Rwandan gendarmes led by an able commander who was evidently not caught up in the tribal violence. The gendarmes assisted the Americans by providing escorts for movement around the city.

The emergency evacuation plan called for a departure either from the airport or overland by road to Burundi. Pamela telephoned the U.S. Embassy in Burundi and spoke to the RSO there. He volunteered to drive north toward the border to check on conditions outside Kigali. Meanwhile, Pamela established an open line with the State Department and Colonel Kalinowski did the same with U.S. military officials at the U.S. European Command (USEUCOM) in Stuttgart, Germany. They also discussed evacuation plans

Several Embassy homes were ransacked by Rwandan looters.

with members of other Western embassies. Jack destroyed the cryptographic equipment and assembled the radios that the Americans would need. Andrew O'Dwyer, who had no security clearance of any kind, went to work destroying classified files. Anticipating the possibility of an overland escape, Jack and Andrew also filled the Embassy vehicles with gasoline as best they could.

Both Colonel Kalinowski and Pamela were able to leave the Embassy and meet with Rwandan Government officials on Friday, seeking assurances that U.S. citizens would not be fired on. At one point they met also with Canadian General Dallaire, the senior UN officer in Kigali, who offered his assistance in the evacuation. Pamela reported these developments to the Ambassador by radio.

In their discussions with Colonel Kalinowski, USEUCOM officials offered to send a reinforced company of U.S. Marines to help get the Americans out of Kigali by way of the airport. The Marines also could provide helicopter gunship cover for an overland route, EUCOM officials added. A third option was to leave overland without a U.S. military escort. The four Americans reviewed the options for the Ambassador in a Friday afternoon radio call.

"Sir," Colonel Kalinowski told Rawson. "I think trying to get to the airport is a bad idea. Even though it's a short distance, we'd have to pass through some of the worst fighting and there is no way to guarantee that our convoys will not be fired on." Colonel Kalinowski pointed out also that the Marines were not familiar with Kigali; it was very unlikely that any spoke the local dialect and few if any were likely to be fluent in French. If either of the warring factions mistook their attempts to evacuate the Americans for assistance to one side or the other, the situation might become worse. Finally, the Bujumbura RSO's reconnaissance revealed no signs of unrest between the Burundi border and the southern outskirts of Kigali.

"We'll go overland," the Ambassador told Colonel Kalinowski and Pamela. "Thank EUCOM for their offer, but tell them we don't need the Marines to come into Kigali. We'll link up with them in Bujumbura."

The overland option in the evacuation plan called for the Americans in and around Kigali to gather at previously designated assembly points—depending on where they lived—and leave in three convoys, heading west out of Kigali and turning south to Burundi. Those located outside the Kigali area would take other overland routes to Burundi, Zaire, or Tanzania.

The Ambassador reached his decision around 1500 hours on Friday, too late for an assembly and departure that day. He told Colonel Kalinowski and Pamela to implement the evacuation plan beginning on Saturday morning. By this point, Americans were calling into the Embassy from locations all over the city, seeking help and advice. Pamela passed the word through the warden system. She learned that one of the women in a missionary group was now in labor and began searching for a qualified physician to help.

Saturday, 9 April

On Saturday morning, Americans from different parts of the city began to assemble at their assigned areas. Lew Giordano, a State Department communicator who had been able to join the others at the Embassy, drove an Embassy van into parts of the city marked by heavy fighting to help bring the Americans to safety. At times, Rwandan gendarmes were able to escort Giordano. At other times he went alone. General Dallaire used his contacts to get RPF assurance that U.S. convoys would not be attacked.

Pamela and Colonel Kalinowski passed the word for the Americans to place a U.S. flag or a white flag on their vehicles as a sign of neutrality. They wanted to avoid having the three convoys bunch up at the roadblocks, which now dotted all of the routes out of Kigali, so they timed the departure of each one to phase the evacuation. The first convoy left its assembly point at 1230 hours on Saturday. Citizens from several other Western nations, including Canada, Germany, and Switzerland, joined the Americans and swelled the size of the convoys. Once out of Kigali, the Americans saw no sign of the carnage that marked the fighting inside the city. As they crossed the border with Burundi, U.S. officials were able to check off their names using Pamela's list of U.S. personnel.

The last convoy, led by Ambassador Rawson (who spoke the local dialect fluently) and the DCM, left Kigali around 1300 hours on Saturday. This convoy consisted of 108

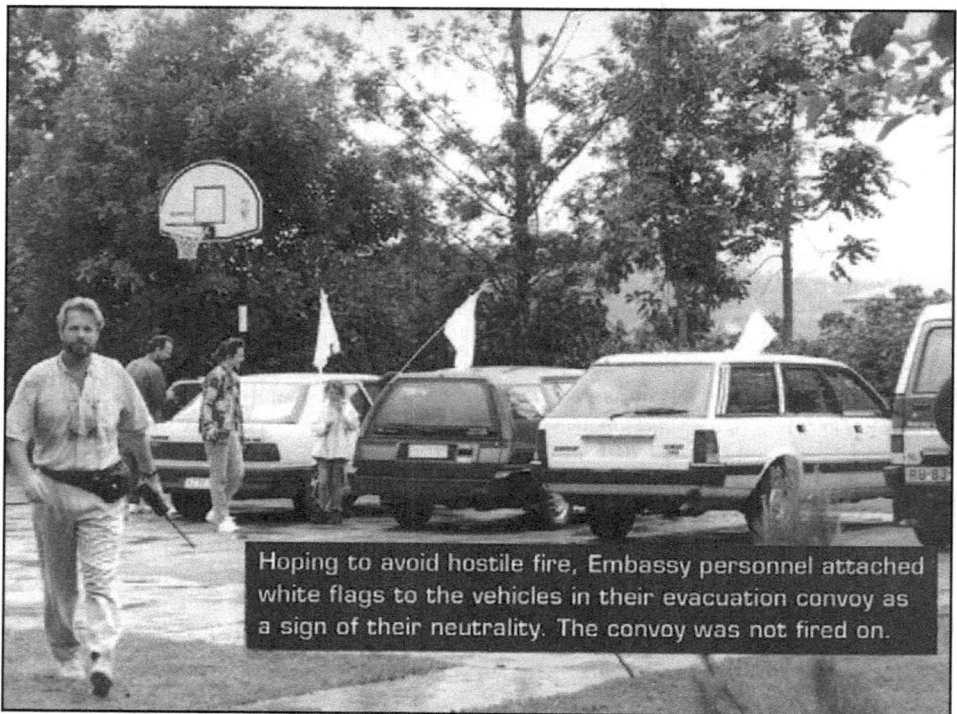

Hoping to avoid hostile fire, Embassy personnel attached white flags to the vehicles in their evacuation convoy as a sign of their neutrality. The convoy was not fired on.

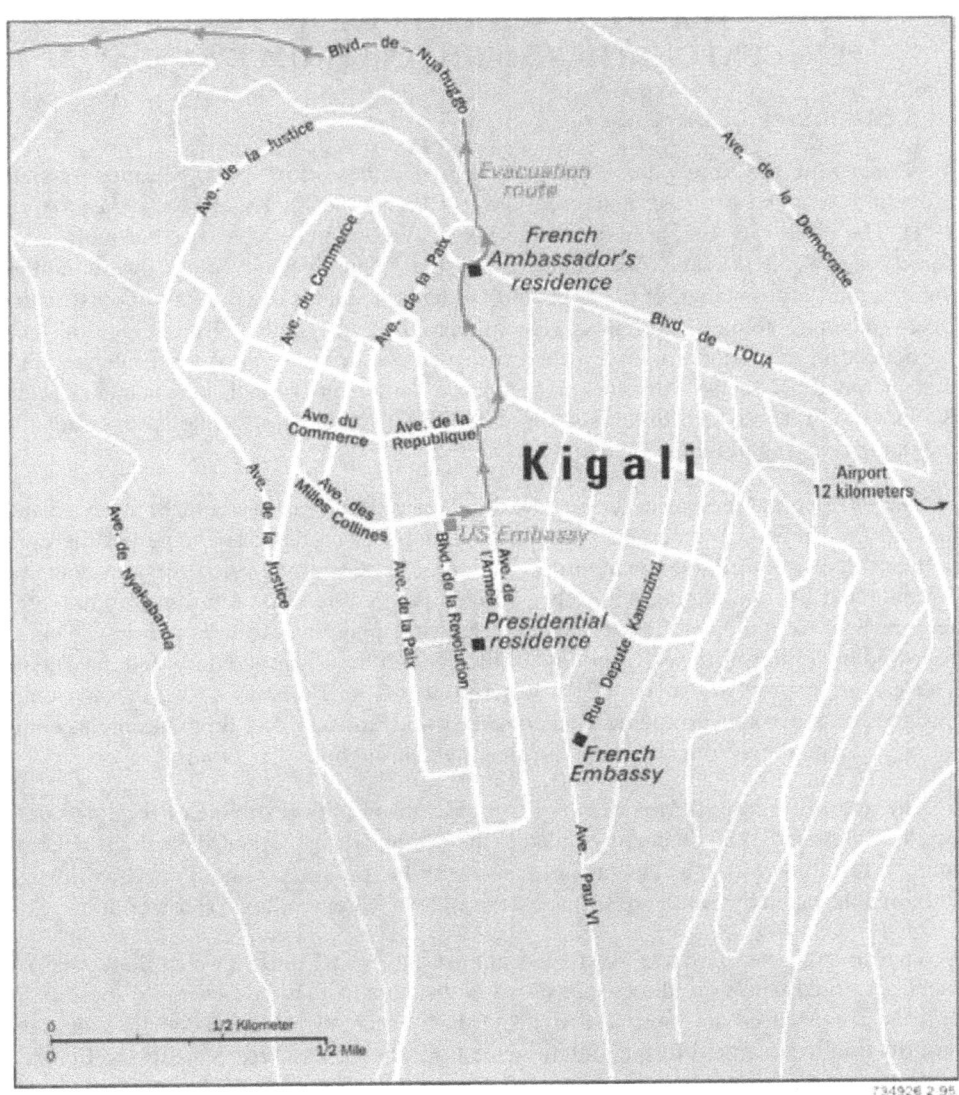

Site of US Embassy, Kigali. The Embassy compound consists of a two-story concrete Chancery building and a USIA cultural center adjoining it.

vehicles carrying more than 600 people, only nine of them Americans. All 258 Americans residing in Rwanda either left on one of the convoys or were accounted for, a few choosing to remain behind and leave with the Belgian and French evacuations later.

TEACHING NOTE FOR USE WITH "EVACUATING THE AMERICANS FROM RWANDA"

A Summary of the Case

"Evacuating the Americans From Rwanda" describes efforts by U.S. Embassy staff officers to respond to the dramatic collapse of civil order in Kigali, Rwanda in April 1994. The small U.S. Embassy faced the task of evacuating or otherwise accounting for some 258 U.S. citizens at a time when extremist Hutu gunmen and soldiers were indulging in a murderous slaughter of Tutsis and moderate Hutus. The main protagonist in the case—a young female foreign service officer given the name "Pamela Smith"—is introduced in the first paragraph, followed by a brief description of the Embassy staff that included a Defense Attache (a U.S. Army lieutenant colonel, here named "Mike Kalinowski.") These two officers—supported by several others—later proved instrumental in carrying out the evacuation.

The opening paragraphs describe how Smith carried out her assignment to revise and expand the Embassy's emergency action plan and sets up the early stages of the civil collapse that followed the apparent destruction of an aircraft carrying the presidents of Rwanda and Burundi, along with other African political leaders, returning from a conference held to find a solution to the tribal violence plaguing Rwandan society. This is followed by a brief historical overview of the conflict between the Hutus and the Tutsis. The early paragraphs also include a description of the Embassy's "warden system," designed to maintain communications between the Embassy and the widespread community of Americans, most of them missionaries, throughout the country.

The rest of the case study is a day-by-day description of the evolving crisis and of how Smith, Kalinowski, and others responded to the extreme danger it posed for the U.S. community, resulting within a few days in a successful evacuation without any U.S. losses. Photographs taken by Smith are sprinkled through the case, lending a sense of drama.

The research for "Rwanda" consisted almost entirely of interviews of State Department personnel who were directly involved in the actual situation. Several of these individuals are referred to by pseudonyms; others, such as Ambassador Rawson, are described in true name. Finished intelligence from the CIA's Directorate of Intelligence provided the background for the historical parts of the case study. The case was coordinated within the Foreign Service Institute (FSI) and with Ambassador Rawson, who offered several useful suggestions.

Intended Context

Rwanda was written for a State Department Foreign Service Institute (FSI) course entitled "The Security Overseas Seminar," and is intended to support a 60-minute discussion. The purpose of this case is to capture the value of the Rwandan experience, describing the preparations that Smith and others took before the crisis exploded, and how they responded once the rampaging mobs took control of Kigali. Instructors using this case at FSI have experienced no difficulty focusing students' attention on these issues, particularly in view of the unusually dramatic nature of the events described. In addition to the "nuts-and-bolts" details of Smith's preparations, the case may also be used to draw students' attention to broader issues, including the leadership characteristics that Smith demonstrated during the crisis, including foresight, personal courage, and acceptance of responsibility for the safety of those in her care.

Teaching Objectives

Students who discuss this case study should be able to:

- Describe in detail specific steps that State Department personnel should take in anticipation of the possibility that an emergency evacuation may be required. This description should include noting the importance of planning, coordination, and system testing; an awareness of where all of the prospective evacuees are located and how to contact them; how to coordinate with prospective sources of assistance, such as U.S. military forces; and how to keep State Department headquarters personnel informed.

- Describe in detail how to respond effectively to the outbreak of civil violence once it begins. An effective response to crisis would include the establishment of a communications center; keeping an accurate record of events as they occur; liaison with local or other authority; the destruction of classified material; and others as determined by the instructor.

- Identify those elements of leadership that comprise an effective response to a physically dangerous crisis.

A Suggested Teaching Plan

It is often helpful to begin a class by asking for a volunteer to describe Pamela Smith. This is an easy question to answer and gets the group accustomed to speaking in response to questions rather than waiting for the lecture that most students invariably anticipate. No more than five minutes should be devoted to discussing Smith; keeping the descriptive terms on a flipchart or on a side-board if one is available. This part of the discussion is mostly a "warm-up;" instructors are unlikely to need to refer to it in detail later.

The first block of analysis—which should require about 20 minutes—focuses on Smith's preparations before the crisis occurred. In this block, students should concentrate on her initiative and planning skills. Perceptive students will note that Smith went well beyond what was required in terms of detail in her emergency action plan, making a concerted effort to contact each individual personally and keeping a record of their whereabouts, passport numbers, dates of birth, next of kin, their photographs, and other personal data in a file held at Smith's home. Some students have criticized this practice as potentially dangerous; terrorists looking for a list of Americans to use as hostages would easily be able to exploit such data.

As students volunteer various specific acts, probing questions can explore how each specific step of preparation helped Smith once the slaughter began. For example, in answer to the general question regarding preparations, a student typically will cite the network of contacts that Pamela built up in the months before the crisis. Probing questions might include, "How exactly did that pay off for her? What attitudes did she portray with these contacts? How did the various Rwandan factions respond to her when she sought assurances of their neutrality? Why did they respond this way?"

One specific step students often cite is the establishment of the warden system, and practice with its functioning. "What are the pros and cons of such a system?" an instructor might ask. "Were there other ways in which communication could have been accomplished, or rumors corrected?" In Rwanda, the warden system relied on high-frequency radios, as the telephone system was unreliable and undeveloped. In fact, the telephone system broke down during the crisis, and the Ambassador could not communicate except by radio. A probing question during consideration of the warden system would be to explore how such a system would work in a country in which there were thousands of U.S. evacuees, not just a few hundred.

When using this case study with FSI students, it has proved helpful to ask groups to describe their own experience with emergency action plans, warden systems, and so on. Many have interesting and colorful stories to relate.

As a second block of analysis, one may focus the discussion on Smith's conduct before and during the crisis. A bridging question to this block might be something like, "What does [that step of preparation] tell us about her?" During this part of the discussion—which should take about 20 minutes—students have an opportunity to examine how Smith's conduct reflects some basic characteristics of leadership. At numerous points during this crisis, Smith could easily have retreated to the comparative safety of her apartment and kept out of sight. Her conduct amply demonstrated exceptional courage and a strong sense of personal responsibility, both hallmarks of a leader. Further, in calmly counseling the increasingly terrified Americans who called in to her for information, Smith also demonstrated the ability to mask her own fear—which was certainly present—on behalf of others. Smith was not alone in this, of course. Kalinowski, Giordano, and others also behaved courageously. After the crisis was resolved, Smith was awarded the State Department's highest decoration for courage.

Turning for a moment to the role of "devil's advocate," instructors may wish to ask if the students think Smith took on too much responsibility, making decisions that ordinarily would have been made by the Ambassador. Some students may indeed advance this view, while others will counter that Smith was carrying out the Ambassador's intent at a time when the Ambassador himself could not safely leave his compound to take command of the situation; therefore the authority that Smith asserted was consistent with the emergency. (Rawson himself shares the latter view.) About 10 minutes on this question should be enough.

In a five-minute summary, instructors may wish to highlight the elaborate preparations that Smith took in anticipation of the crisis. As the junior member of the emergency action committee, she could easily have satisfied the requirements of her assignment with less attention to detail. (Many FSI students can cite examples of this approach to emergency action planning.) She chose, however, to tackle an unpopular job with enthusiasm and skill, and when the plan was tested by the dramatic events described in the case, her efforts paid off handsomely.

THE BOMBING OF THE MARINE BARRACKS IN BEIRUT, 23 OCTOBER 1983[3]

At 0622 hours on Sunday, 23 October 1983, an unidentified young man drove a yellow Mercedes Benz stakebed truck into a parking lot of the Beirut International Airport. Accelerating toward the four-story concrete building that housed the headquarters elements of a U.S. Marine Corps Battalion Landing Team (BLT), the man drove through a barbed wire and concertina fence and passed between two Marine guard posts without being engaged by fire. The truck then passed through an open gate and around some sewer pipe barriers, flattened the Sergeant of the Guard's sandbagged booth, and entered the lobby of the building. The driver then detonated a bomb loaded on the truck.

The explosion—roughly equivalent to that of some 12,000 lbs of TNT—lifted the building from its concrete pillar foundation. The building then collapsed, killing 241 of its estimated 350 occupants. It was the largest single-day loss of life in the Marine Corps since the Battle of Iwo Jima.

Lebanon: A Troubled History

The modern state of Lebanon was created after World War I, when France combined territories seized from the defeated Ottoman Empire with land the French already held in the eastern Mediterranean region known as the Levant. The population of the new state included several groups of different religions, including Maronite Christians, Greek Orthodox Christians, Druze, Sunni and Shiite Muslims, and others. The non-Maronite groups in particular were opposed to integration into the new state, but as French colonial forces retreated during World War II, the Maronites and the Shiite Muslims struck a bargain that evidently was acceptable to most Lebanese. Known as the "National Pact of 1943," the bargain allocated political power on the basis of the sectarian balance reflected in the census of 1932. According to this agreement, the president and commander of the armed forces would always be Maronites; the prime minister would be a Sunni Muslim; the speaker of the chamber of deputies would be a Shiite; and for every five non-Christian deputies there would be six Christians.

In addition to divisions based on religious faith, Lebanese politics was marked by complex local associations based on sectarian and clan relationships. Nearly constant quarrels among local chieftains frequently paralyzed the weak central government; private militias

---

[3] This case study is based mainly on the "Report of the DoD Commission on Beirut International Airport Terrorist Act, 23 October 1983;" an unpublished doctoral dissertation written by Dr. Jack Matthews (Lt.Col., USMC, Ret.); and on interviews with Marines who were directly involved in the events described. The case study was written in September 1997 by Col. Thomas W. Shreeve, USMCR. Photos are courtesy of USMC combat camera teams. This, and all cases and case studies, may be used with the permission of Tom Shreeve. He is available at (703) 237-4624 or at *tomshreeve@aol.com.*

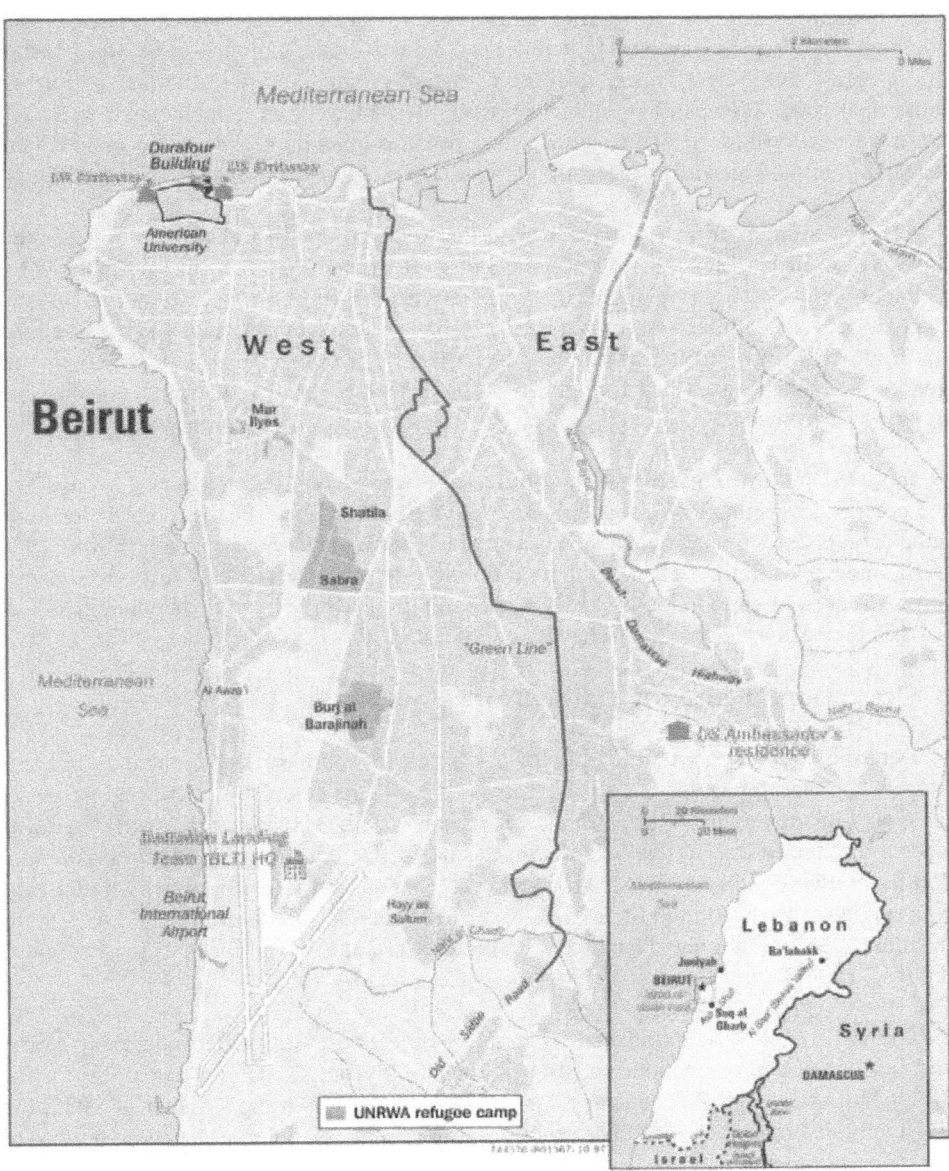

Beirut, 1983.

were common. Over the years after World War II, the political balance struck by the National Pact became increasingly unrepresentative of the population as the Muslim groups grew significantly faster than the Christian groups. To cloud the picture further, more than 100,000 Palestinian refugees arrived in 1948, after the establishment of Israel; these were followed in 1971 by another wave of Palestinian immigration that included the leadership of the Palestinian Liberation Organization (PLO) from Jordan.

The Palestinians formed alliances with dissident groups in Lebanon and used their bases in southern Lebanon for sporadic raids into Israel. From about the late 1960s, Lebanese society became increasingly polarized, with Maronite Christians mostly opposing the Palestinians' activities and Muslims generally supporting them. Israel had for some years favored the Maronites, and after the arrival of the PLO, Israeli intelligence and security services forged closer links to the various Maronite militias and other power centers.

In 1975, civil disunity in Lebanon broke into war among the competing groups and the central government of Lebanon essentially ceased to exist. Fearing that Palestinian attacks on Israel would provoke an unwanted war between Syria and Israel, in June 1976 Syria intervened in the Lebanese conflict on the side of the Maronite Christians, despite Syria's record of support to the PLO. Active fighting subsided and a stalemate resulted, leaving the basic issues of the Lebanese conflict unresolved.

Operation "Peace for Galilee"

Determined to deprive the PLO of its bases in southern Lebanon and install a Maronite government that would be consistent with its interests in the region, Israel invaded Lebanon with 70,000 troops on 6 June 1982. The invasion—referred to as Operation "Peace for Galilee"—brought the Israeli Defense Force (IDF) into potential conflict with Syrian Army units stationed in Lebanon and risked a wider Middle East war, an outcome the United States was eager to avoid. Despite the risk, the IDF pressed its attack and within a few days linked up with a Christian force known as the Phalange, led by Bashir Gemayel.

The IDF quickly accomplished its military objectives: PLO Chairman Yasir Arafat and his forces were surrounded in Beirut, and the Syrian air defense capability in the Shouf Mountains and Bekaa Valley was crippled. Throughout the summer of 1982, the IDF continued to tighten the noose around Beirut. Members of the news media flocked to the beleaguered city and began daily coverage of Israeli attacks against PLO strongholds in West Beirut. Graphic images of destruction reached media audiences in the United States and elsewhere as Israeli air and artillery units pounded targets in heavily populated portions of the city.

The Governments of Egypt, Saudi Arabia, and Jordan publicly blamed the United States for failing to restrain the Israeli attacks. European governments soon echoed these claims and threatened to apply economic sanctions against Israel. In the United States, the Reagan administration worried about the possibility of Soviet intervention to assist the USSR's longtime Syrian ally.

A U.S. Plan

Frustrated by mounting foreign and domestic objections to Israeli attacks on population centers in West Beirut, President Reagan in August 1982 accepted a Lebanese Government proposal to lead a multinational force that would extract the PLO from Beirut and oversee the return to Syria of Syrian Army units. Other stakeholders, including the Israelis and the PLO, communicated their acceptance of an "intercession force" as long as it was led by the United States. On 20 August, Reagan announced that agreement had been reached among the governments of the United States, Lebanon, France, Italy, and Israel and with the PLO to plan for the safe departure from Beirut of PLO leaders, administrative offices, and combatants as well as certain remaining elements of the Syrian Army.

On 25 August 1982, some 800 Marines and sailors of the 32nd Marine Amphibious Unit (MAU) landed in Beirut as part of a multinational peacekeeping force that was to oversee the evacuation of the PLO and the Syrian Army units that remained in Beirut. The multinational force consisted of 400 French and 800 Italian troops in addition to the U.S. contingent. (A limited number of British troops later joined the effort.) Some 15,000 Palestinians and Syrians were quickly and safely evacuated from Beirut by sea or over the Shouf Mountains. The operation—led by Marine Col. James M. Mead—was widely regarded as a success.

One of the keys to the speedy evacuation was PLO acceptance of an assurance detailed in the so-called "Departure Plan" that protected Palestinian noncombatants left behind in the PLO camps:

- Law-abiding Palestinian noncombatants left behind in Beirut, including the families of those of who have departed, will be subject to Lebanese laws and regulations. The Governments of Lebanon and the United States will provide appropriate guarantees in the following ways:

  - The Lebanese Government will provide its guarantees on the basis of having secured assurances from armed groups with which it has been in touch.

  - The United States will provide its assurances received from the Government of Israel and the leadership of certain Lebanese groups with which it has been in touch.

On 10 September, its mission apparently accomplished, the U.S. contingent departed. Its departure evidently came as a surprise to the French and Italian forces, which then also prepared to leave. U.S. Special Envoy Philip Habib—who led the U.S. team that negotiated the ceasefire and the PLO withdrawal—did not inform Marine commanders of the guarantee he had made to the PLO assuring the safety of the Palestinian noncombatants who remained behind in Beirut.

Most of Beirut's population appeared to welcome the arrival of the Marines in September 1982.

The Plan Unravels

On 14 September, President-elect Bashir Gemayel was assassinated by unidentified assailants who detonated a car bomb outside his Phalange headquarters. The IDF immediately redeployed into positions surrounding Beirut. On the night of 16 September, members of the Christian Phalange militia group entered two Palestinian refugee camps at Shabra and Shatilla near the Beirut International Airport. Inside the camps over the next day and a half, Phalange forces slaughtered an estimated 800 Palestinian women, children, and men over military age.

The U.S. public reacted with shock and outrage, particularly as evidence emerged of Israeli complicity in the atrocity. On 20 September, President Reagan directed the Chairman of the Joint Chiefs of Staff to provide a contingent to participate in a new multinational peacekeeping force. The Governments of France and Italy quickly agreed to take part in a renewed effort. "The participation of the American forces in Lebanon will again be for a limited period," Reagan stated. "But I have concluded that there is no alternative to their returning to Lebanon if that country is to have a chance to stand on its own two feet."

The second U.S. involvement was again assigned to the Marine Corps, and on the morning of 29 September, Colonel Mead and his Marines arrived in Beirut to take on a new mission. This was: to establish an environment which will permit the Lebanese Armed Forces to carry out their responsibilities in the Beirut area. When directed, USCINCEUR will introduce U.S. forces as a part of a multinational force presence in the Beirut area to occupy and secure positions along a designated section of the line south of the Beirut International Airport to a position in the vicinity of the presidential palace; be prepared to protect U.S. forces; and, on order, conduct retrograde operations as required.

To this mission President Reagan on 28 October added National Security Decision Directive (NSDD) 64, which established as a U.S. objective the withdrawal of all foreign forces from Lebanon by not later than the end of calendar year 1982. The NSDD also suggested that the U.S. Multinational Force (USMNF) might not be withdrawn until the Government of Lebanon could once again control, administer, and defend its sovereign territory.

Command Relationships: Strong Chain or Tangled Web?

By the 1980s, Lebanon was under the operational jurisdiction of the U.S. European Command, known as EUCOM, led by U.S. Army Gen. Bernard W. Rogers (designated USCINCEUR) and headquartered in Stuttgart. The EUCOM commander normally delegated amphibious operations to his naval subordinate, known as CINCUSNAVEUR, who in September 1982 was U.S. Navy Vice Adm. Ronald J. Hays, headquartered in London. From Admiral Hays, command authority was delegated according to doctrine to the commander of the Navy's Sixth Fleet (COMSIXTHFLT), Vice Adm. William H. Rowden, USN.

Admiral Rowden exercised command over a Mediterranean Amphibious Ready Group (MARG) that was continuously available for regional assignments. The MARG consisted of a naval squadron of between three and five ships and an 1800-man Marine Amphibious Unit (MAU) embarked aboard the ships. The MARG was commanded by U.S. Navy Capt. Richard F. White. (In accordance with naval custom, Captain White was referred to as Commodore for the purposes of this assignment.)

Commodore White became Commander of Task Force 61 (CTF 61) and commander of the amphibious task force (CATF) for the purposes of the U.S. mission in Lebanon. Colonel Mead, as commander of the MAU, became commander of the landing force (CLF), subordinate to Commodore White. Colonel Mead was also designated Commander of Task Force 62 (CTF 62) and Commander, U.S. Forces Ashore, Lebanon. Colonel Mead's communications capability enabled him to communicate with CTF 61 but not directly with COMSIXTHFLT.

These command relationships were based on longstanding amphibious doctrine and were thoroughly understood by the naval, Marine, and other commanders involved in the operation. The apparent clarity of these relationships soon became clouded, however, as various commands outside the immediate area became increasingly eager to play an active role in the U.S. effort and advanced a variety of interests.

On 21 September, about a week before Colonel Mead's return as commander of the MAU, a 14-member U.S. military liaison team arrived in Beirut to assess the conditions of the Lebanese Armed Forces (LAF) and recommend ways to improve its effectiveness.

The 32nd MAU Executive Officer negotiated the use of the building that became the BLT Headquarters in September 1982.

The team was led by U.S. Army Maj. Gen. Gerald T. Bartlett. The team's "Bartlett Report" resulted in the creation of the U.S. Office of Military Cooperation (OMC), led by U.S. Army Col. Thomas Fintel. Colonel Fintel arrived in Lebanon with an official "Terms of Reference" from the Chairman of the Joint Chiefs of Staff that designated Fintel as the senior U.S. military representative in Lebanon. In an interview conducted years after the operation, Colonel Fintel stated that at the time of his assignment he considered himself senior to the MAU commander.

The continued high intensity of U.S. media attention to the peacekeeping effort appeared to provoke corresponding levels of interest in various U.S. commands that proceeded to exercise considerable influence on operational matters in Beirut. For example, in October 1982 the MAU began patrolling portions of East Beirut in response to a request from the Government of Lebanon and approved by the U.S. Secretary of Defense. The MAU commander by this time was Col. Thomas M. Stokes. (See exhibit 1 for a summary of the MAU commanders' respective tenures). Colonel Stokes developed a plan for patrolling and—convinced that the environment had become reasonably benign—ordered his men not to wear their helmets and flak jackets out of concern for their image as peacekeepers. When a photograph of a Marine patrol appeared in the *Washington Post* in early November, the MAU received a message from Fleet Marine Force Atlantic headquarters in Norfolk, Virginia, directing the Marines to wear their full combat equipment.

Senior commands soon felt a need to establish their own presence in Beirut. For example, over the course of the peacekeeping mission a number of different Marine officers were assigned as EUCOM liaison officers. While in Lebanon, these officers were stationed at the U.S. Embassy and had secure-voice satellite communications capability that enabled them to communicate directly to Stuttgart, London, or Washington, DC. Soon after the return of the MAU in late September, the EUCOM liaison officer began attending daily meetings of the so-called Military Coordinating Committee, chaired by the chief of staff of the LAF and including the commanders of the multinational forces present in Lebanon. The MAU executive officer attended these meetings, but apparently by common consent was regarded as a junior partner. Meetings of a similar group called the Political Coordinating Committee were attended by the ambassadors from the nations represented in the multinational force. CINCEUR's military representative attended the meetings of this committee as the senior U.S. military voice. According to a detailed report on U.S. involvement in Lebanon, the MAU commander was never invited to attend the meetings of this committee.

The Chairman of the Joint Chiefs of Staff (U.S. Army Gen. John Vessey) soon assigned his own liaison officer to Beirut. By the summer of 1983, this officer was U.S. Army Gen. Carl W. Steiner, who was equipped with an independent satellite communications capability that enabled him to speak directly to General Vessey in the Pentagon, something Steiner did regularly. Queried years later as to the need for this direct line of communication, General Steiner said:

Now the reason for this is there was a perception in Washington that the reporting through the chain of command…was constipated, and [senior commanders in

Washington] were not getting the picture…on a timely basis of the details, the evidence, the facts upon which to make appropriate decisions. And many times the Joint Chiefs would make a decision and send it through appropriate channels, through [CINCEUR] and on down, and I would get a call [from Washington], "You tell me how it comes out at the other end and how long it takes to get there."

The Mission of "Presence"

Marine and Navy commanders and staff officers were aware that the mission of "presence" cited in the initiating directive was novel and difficult to define. When the MAU returned to Beirut in late September 1982, however, the population of the city, evidently exhausted by the civil conflict and the rigors of Operation Peace for Galilee, appeared to welcome the Marines' return as a respite. The apparent vagueness of "presence" went unchallenged at all levels of command involved in the operation.

Before the Marines went ashore in late September, a U.S. team made up of Ambassador Morris Draper and Lt.Col. Charles R. Smith, the executive officer of the 32nd MAU, met with members of the Lebanese Government and senior IDF commanders to agree on the exact location of the Marines' headquarters in the Beirut area. According to an earlier agreement reached between Ambassador Draper and Israeli Defense Minister Ariel Sharon, the Marines were given control of the Beirut International Airport (BIA) while the IDF continued to exercise control of the Old Sidon Road, which passed east of the BIA and then north, eventually intersecting with the Beirut-Damascus Highway. IDF officers insisted that they needed the Old Sidon Road in order to supply their units in the Shouf Mountains, east of the airport. Colonel Mead reportedly accepted this arrangement, in part because he believed that Marine control of the road risked the perception—particularly among Muslim factions—that the MAU was protecting an important IDF supply line.

Draper and Smith agreed to house the 32nd MAU's commander and his small staff in what had once been the fire-fighting school at the BIA. The BLT headquarters, they further agreed, would be the much larger building that had been the headquarters of the Lebanese Civil Aviation Authority. Smith reported to Mead that the building selected to house the BLT was structurally sound—it had been successfully used by the PLO, the Syrian Army, and finally the IDF. Mead accepted Smith's evaluation, and the BLT moved into the building. When Colonel Stokes relieved Mead in early November, Stokes, commanding the 24th MAU, did not see a reason to change the location of the BLT headquarters.

Pursuing what he regarded as the mission of "presence," MAU commander Stokes ordered his Marines to develop a patrol plan, and on 4 November 1982, the MAU began its first motorized patrols. Initially the patrols appeared to be welcomed in the neighborhoods of East and West Beirut and Stokes quickly expanded their scope, sending patrols well into the outlying suburbs. The success of these patrols led Stokes to consider expanding them further, and on 5 December—despite the original agreement with the IDF—the Marines began patrolling the Old Sidon Road. Although they encountered no obstructions, within a week CINCEUR ordered patrolling on the Old Sidon Road to cease, citing concerns that it could give the impression that the MAU was assisting the IDF.

The apparent vagueness of the mission went unchallenged at all levels of command.

The Marines on Liberty

Almost as soon as they arrived, the Marines began expanding their social contacts in Beirut, organizing "liberty runs," for example, to and from the Christian resort town of Juniyah, just north of Beirut. (These were terminated in November out of concern for the impression they might cause among Muslims.) With permission from the U.S. Embassy, on 10 November the Marines celebrated their Corps' birthday at an upscale restaurant in East Beirut. According to a Marine lieutenant colonel who was present, not one Muslim had been invited. In early December, a group of about 50 Marines were the guests of a group of prominent Lebanese at another East Beirut restaurant. Again, they had sought and received U.S. Embassy permission to attend the function, which was a banquet honoring wounded veterans of the LAF. Fadi Frem, the leader of the Christian Phalange, was the guest of honor. Photographs of the Marines attending the banquet were published in a local newspaper. At Christmas, many Christian Lebanese families hosted Marines in private homes, while a Christian Lebanese arms dealer named Joseph Sfair hosted a party for about 100 Marine officers at the exclusive Tabarhja Hotel.

Signs of Growing Hostility

In late 1982, Marine Capt. Charles Johnson commanded a company of Marines assigned to a sector around the Lebanese Riehan College complex. He attended a daily commanders' conference at the BLT headquarters building, and to get from the Riehan College to the BIA he had to travel through a Shiite enclave known as Hayy es Salaam, a neighborhood the Marines patrolled routinely and that initially appeared to be friendly. Captain Johnson reported that around mid-December 1982 he began to notice a subtle but unmistakable shift in the mood of the local population while on his daily excursion to and from the BIA. He noticed the presence of more young men; then he and his driver began to receive unfriendly glares, and then verbal taunts. Soon he began to be followed as he drove through the narrow streets. He caught glimpses of weapons and began to see posters that featured Iran's Ayatol-lah Khomeini.

In mid-January 1983, intense fighting erupted between the Druze and members of the Christian militia, and Israeli casualties mounted among troops assigned to patrol the Old Sidon Road. In mid-February 1983, Colonel Mead returned again to Beirut as commander of a unit now designated the 22nd MAU; by this point the Old Sidon Road and the area immediately to the east had been reduced to rubble. Within a few days, five of Mead's Marines were wounded in the first direct attack on the U.S. peacekeepers as a 12-man patrol passed through the southern suburb of Ouzai. A group calling itself "Islamic Jihad" claimed credit for the attack, according to media reports. On 16 March, another five Marines were wounded in a grenade attack while patrolling in the city.

On 18 April, a large car-bomb exploded outside the U.S. Embassy in Beirut, killing 61 persons including 17 Americans. Islamic Jihad again claimed credit for the attack. British Ambassador Sir David Roberts immediately offered working spaces in the British Embassy for the U.S. political, military, and consular sections, an offer the Americans accepted. Other U.S. Embassy functions moved into a building known as the Durafour Building in Beirut. U.S.CINCEUR General Rogers promptly directed Mead to provide security for the British Embassy, the Durafour Building, and for U.S. Ambassador Robert Dillon at his residence.

The security duties assigned to the MAU resulted in a change to the Rules of Engage-ment (ROE) issued to the Marines in Beirut. While guarding the British Embassy, the Durafour Building, or the Ambassador's residence, Marines were provided with ROE that were significantly more permissive than those that prevailed at the BLT headquarters. Those on duty at BIA were not permitted to have a magazine inserted into their rifles, apparently out of concern for the possibility of accidental discharges that might result in Lebanese or other casualties. In numerous cases, the same individuals were sometimes on guard duty at the secured locations and sometimes at BIA.

In spite of these signs of rising hostility to the U.S. efforts in Beirut, there was no change to the basic "presence" mission of the Marines. U.S. Army Col. Ralph Hallenbeck—then chief of current operations in the J-3 section of CINCEUR headquarters in Stuttgart—was assigned the duty of monitoring daily activities in Lebanon for General Rogers. Asked why General Rogers did not amend the MAU's mission in light of the U.S. Embassy bombing, Hallenbeck stated, "CINCEUR's headquarters staff viewed the attack as an isolated inci-dent [directed] against the United States; it was seen as a peripheral event not reflecting local or popular opposition; and finally, it was not seen as related to the basic mission of peacekeeping."

The US Embassy was attacked in April 1983. The bombing left 61 dead, including 17 Americans.

On 30 May, Col. Timothy Geraghty and the 24th MAU took over from Colonel Mead. Geraghty's BLT commander was Lt. Col. Larry Gerlach. On 8 June, according to interviews conducted later, IDF tanks fired some 100 rounds of 105mm ammunition into Hayy es Salaam, the Muslim neighborhood near the Marine positions around the BIA. Confronted by a Marine officer, the IDF tank commander claimed that he ordered his tanks to fire because someone in the enclave had fired a rocket at the Israelis. The IDF commander added, "We are firing at the village because we have no respect for the Lebanese. We like to see them run."

On 15 July, Lieutenant Colonel Gerlach modified the ROE for Marines on guard at the BIA. Those who manned "external posts" were now allowed to keep a loaded magazine in their rifles but could not chamber a round. Those who manned "internal posts" remained under the original ROE and were required to keep their magazines in pouches they carried on their belts. The ROE for the Marines guarding the British Embassy, the Durafour Building, and the Ambassador's residence remained the least restrictive.

On 10 and 11 August, an estimated 35 rounds of mortar and rocket fire fell on Marine positions, wounding one Marine. On 28 August, the Marines returned fire for the first time. On 29 August, Marine artillery silenced Druze guns after two Marines were killed in a mortar attack. The same day, Marines of Company A engaged in a four-hour gun battle with a militia group from inside Hayy es Salaam, an area they had once regarded as friendly and under their protection. Two Marines were killed and 14 were wounded. There was no change to the mission of the MAU and no fundamental shift in its composition or defensive posture.

In early September, a Druze force reportedly reinforced by PLO fighters routed a Christian element of the LAF in the high ground overlooking the BIA. Marine positions were subjected to sporadic indirect fire over the next few weeks. On 16 September, U.S. forces employed naval gunfire in response to shelling of the U.S. Ambassador's residence and Marine positions at the airport. On 19 September, as LAF troops fought with Druze forces over the hamlet of Suq al Garb in the Shouf Mountains, the *U.S.S John Rogers* and the *U.S.S Virginia* fired their guns in support of the LAF. According to several observers who were present when Colonel Geraghty received orders to adjust the naval gunfire, Geraghty futilely opposed this action. "Sir, I can't do that," Geraghty was quoted as replying. "That will cost us our neutrality. Do you realize if you do that, we'll get slaughtered down here?"

Security of the BLT Headquarters

In 1983 the BIA was an active international airport servicing an average of 35 flights and 2,400 passengers every day. The airport employed around 1,000 civilians, and ground traffic to and from the area was estimated at about 3,000 vehicles a day. Many vehicles, including large trucks like the one used in the barracks bombing, routinely remained in the airport overnight.

The building chosen as the BLT headquarters was a bombed-out, fire-damaged structure constructed of steel and reinforced concrete. All of the windows on the upper three floors had been replaced with an assortment of plywood, sandbag cloth, and plastic sheeting. The ground floor was an open area enclosed with sandbags and barbed wire.

The building provided excellent protection from the indirect fire that fell on the Marine positions with increasing frequency through the late summer of 1983. Marine casualties throughout the peacekeeping operation were light, and until 23 October, no Marines were killed or wounded in the BLT headquarters building. The roof also provided for excellent observation of the surrounding area, and was ideal as a platform for the wide variety of communications devices employed during the U.S. mission.

When the Marines acquired the building, its apparent caretaker—an elderly Lebanese man the Marines nicknamed "Shuffles" because of his distinctive limp—remained employed in the structure. Shuffles often stayed in the building after normal working hours, sleeping in his office on a cot. After some weeks, he opened a small shop and sold convenience items to the Marines. According to a number of reports, Shuffles was presumed to have died in the explosion, but there was no evidence to establish his death. Subsequent reports suggested that the Marines knew very little about Shuffles, not even his real name.

Throughout the time they used the building, the Marines sought to improve its security, using an estimated 500,000 sandbags and some 10,000 feet of concertina wire. (For a map of the compound and the bomber's route into the central courtyard, see exhibit 2.) The building enabled the various MAUs to centralize logistic support. According to the report of the Long Commission—a group of distinguished senior officers convened by the Secretary of Defense to investigate the bombing—the building was an ideal location for the command post of a battalion actively engaged in fulfilling a peacekeeping and presence mission. The building housed up to 350 personnel, about a fourth of the total command strength. (For more details on the members of the Long Commission, see exhibit 3.)

The Marines of the 24th MAU had four "Alert Conditions," with Alert Condition I representing the highest state of alert. The level of alert was determined by the Combat Operations Center. According to the Long Commission Report, "The security posture on 23 October at the MAU/BLT compound, as described by surviving witnesses, was not in compliance with published directives for Alert Conditions II or III."

The Marines' ROE prohibited them from inserting magazines into their rifles while on interior posts during Alert Conditions II, III, and IV. According to the Long Commission, The MAU commander explained that he made a conscious decision not to permit insertion of magazines in weapons on interior posts to preclude accidental discharge and possible injury to innocent civilians. The threat to the MAU/BLT compound was perceived to be direct and indirect fire, ground attack by personnel, stationary vehicular bombs, and hand grenade/RPG attack. Hostile penetration of the perimeter by cars or trucks was not addressed in the instructions provided the BLT guards.

According to the Long Commission, Colonel Geraghty was "deluged with daily threat information [but] received no specific warning of the time, place, or technique of the 23 October 1983 attack." For example, in the days just before the bombing, the Marines received reports suggesting an imminent car-bomb attack that was said to involve a white Mercedes automobile. Marine CI personnel alerted the MAU to these reports and searched for a car fitting that description.

Colonel Geraghty was not briefed on the details of the bomb that badly damaged the U.S. Embassy the previous April, despite a thorough investigation of the incident by U.S. officials including FBI forensic experts. Further, despite a prolonged series of visits by senior U.S. military and other officials extending up to the eve of the bombing, there was no evidence of any expression of concern over the BLT's security posture nor any recorded suggestion that it be enhanced.

The Morning of 23 October

The Long Commission interviewed many of the Marines who witnessed the bombing. Their reports were corroborative. At around 0500 on 23 October, the sentry on duty at post 6 observed a yellow Mercedes Benz truck entering the parking lot south of the BLT Headquarters building. The truck circled once, then exited to the south. The sentry did not report the truck because it did not stop or appear to be suspicious in any way.

About an hour and 20 minutes later, the same sentry observed a similar truck acceler-ating westward and parallel to the wire barricade. The truck then turned abruptly north, ran over the wire barricade, and accelerated north between posts 6 and 7. The sentry at post 7 heard the truck as it ran over the wire, then observed it and immediately suspected that it was a vehicle bomb. He inserted a magazine into his M-16 rifle, chambered a round and shouldered his weapon. He did not fire, he stated, because by that time the truck was inside the building.

The sentry at post 5 also saw the truck and reported his immediate conclusion that it was a vehicle bomb. He did not have time to react in any way.

The Sergeant of the Guard was facing north or inward and heard the truck as it approached the interior of the building. He later reported that he, too, immediately real-ized that it was hostile. He ran out of his post across the lobby and yelled, "Hit the deck! Hit the deck!" He saw the truck breach the entrance and come to a halt near the center of the lobby. There was a delay of perhaps one or two seconds, he reported, before the actual detonation. (This Marine was badly wounded in the blast.)

When the truck exploded, it created an oblong crater about 30 by 40 feet and nearly nine feet deep. The structure of the building—with a large covered courtyard extending from the lobby floor to the roof—converged the force vectors and greatly intensified the explosion. FBI forensic analysts later described the explosion as the largest conventional blast they had ever seen.

US military personnel and Lebanese rescue workers searched the devastated building for survivors. The blast killed 241 of an estimated 350 occupants.

Study questions:

1. What is your analysis of the reasons for the outcome described in this case study?

2. Do you think the effects of the attack could have been prevented or mitigated? How? Be specific.

3. How do you think responsibility for this event should be allocated?

THE BOMBING OF THE MARINE BARRACKS IN BEIRUT: THE LONG COMMISSION REPORT

In its conclusions, the Long Commission reported that:

■ The combination of a large volume of specific threat warnings that never materialized, and perceived and real pressure to accomplish a unique and difficult mission, contributed significantly to the decisions of the MAU and BLT commanders regarding the security of their force. Nevertheless, the Commission concludes that the security measures in effect in the MAU compound were neither commensurate with the increasing level of threat confronting the USMNF nor sufficient to preclude catastrophic losses such as those that were suffered on the morning of 23 October 1983. The Commission further concludes that while it may have appeared to be an appropriate response to the indirect fire being received, the decision to billet approximately one-quarter of the BLT in a single structure contributed to the catastrophic loss of life.

■ The Commission concludes that the BLT Commander must take responsibility for the concentration of approximately 350 members of his command in the Battalion Headquarters building, thereby providing a lucrative target for attack. Further, the BLT Commander modified prescribed alert procedures, degrading security of the compound.

■ The Commission also concludes that the MAU Commander shares the responsibility for the catastrophic losses in that he condoned the concentration of personnel in the BLT Headquarters building, concurred in modification of prescribed alert procedures, and emphasized safety over security in directing that sentries on Posts 4, 5, 6, and 7 would not load their weapons.

■ The Commission further concludes that although it finds the BLT and MAU Commanders to be at fault, it also finds that there was a series of circumstances beyond their control that influenced their judgment and their actions relating to the security of the USMNF.

Exhibit 1: Periods of Assignment of MAU Commanders in Beirut

Col. James M. Mead, 32nd MAU, 16 August to 10 September 1982 for the evacuation of the PLO and certain units of the Syrian Army.

Col. James M. Mead, 32nd MAU, 29 September to 1 November 1982 during initial stages of the peacekeeping operation.

Col. Thomas M. Stokes, 24th MAU, from 1 November 1982 to 15 February 1983.

Col. James M. Mead, 22nd MAU, from 15 February to 29 May 1983.

Col. Timothy J. Geraghty, 24th MAU, 30 May to 18 November 1983.

Brig. Gen. James R. Joy, 22nd MAU, 19 November 1983 to 9 April 1984.

Taken seconds after detonation, this photograph reveals the magnitude of the blast that FBI investigators called "the largest conventional explosion ever encountered by the US forensics community."

Exhibit 2.

Exhibit 3: Composition of the Long Commission

The five-member "DoD Commission on Beirut International Airport Terrorist Act, 23 October 1983" was established by the Secretary of Defense on 7 November 1983 to conduct a thorough and independent inquiry into all of the facts and circumstances surrounding the 23 October 1983 terrorist attack on the Marine Battalion Landing Team Headquarters at the Beirut International Airport. The Commission was composed of the following five members:

Adm. Robert L. J. Long, USN (Ret.), Chairman

Admiral Long retired as the Commander-in-Chief, Pacific in July 1983, after 40 years of commissioned service that included combat duty in World War II and the Vietnam War. He served in numerous command and staff billets and at the time of his retirement was Vice Chief of Naval Operations.

Honorable Robert J. Murray

Mr. Murray was on the faculty at Harvard University. He was a former Under Secretary of the Navy and former Deputy Assistant Secretary of Defense for International Security Affairs.

Lt. Gen. Joseph T. Palastra, Jr., USA

General Palastra was the Deputy Commander-in-Chief and Chief of Staff, U.S. Pacific Command. He had served in numerous command and staff billets in a career that spanned 29 years of commissioned service.

Lt. Gen. Lawrence F. Snowden, USMC (Ret.)

General Snowden retired as the Chief of Staff, Headquarters, U.S. Marine Corps in May 1979 after 37 years of active service that included combat duty in World War II, Korea, and Vietnam. He served as a regimental commander in Vietnam; Director of the Marine Corps Development Center; Chief of Staff of U.S. Forces, Japan; and Operations Deputy of the Marine Corps with the Joint Chiefs of Staff.

Lt. Gen. Eugene F. Tighe, Jr., USAF (Ret.)

General Tighe retired from the U.S. Air Force as Director of the Defense Intelligence Agency on 1 September 1981 after 39 years of active and reserve Air Force and Army duty.

TEACHING NOTE FOR USE WITH
"THE BOMBING OF THE MARINE BARRACKS IN BEIRUT, 23 OCTOBER 1983"

The Bombing of the Marine Barracks in Beirut, 23 October 1983 is intended for a 75-minute discussion in military training and education courses focused on force protection, counterintelligence, and preparation for command responsibility. The case study also has proved effective for civilian groups, but civilians may need some help understanding some of the terms and relationships unique to the naval service.

A Summary of the Case

This case study is a detailed historical account of a terrorist attack on a Marine Amphibious Unit (MAU) assigned to Beirut, Lebanon in the early 1980s. The case opens with a brief reference to the destructive power of the explosion, which resulted in the deaths of 241 of the estimated 350 occupants of the building that served as the barracks for the MAU. The introductory paragraphs are followed by a brief historical overview of the Lebanese civil war and the political events that provoked U.S. intervention in Lebanon in August 1982. The case describes how U.S. policymakers defined their initially limited objectives in Lebanon, and how these objectives expanded following the widely publicized massacre of Palestinian refugees in mid-September.

The next major section of the case describes the command relationships that prevailed early in the intervention, and how these relationships shifted during the following year. This section is followed by a description of how the Marines interpreted the mission they had been given, and some of their activities—exclusively with the Christian factions of Lebanese society—while not on duty. The case reviews the signs of growing hostility to the Marines' presence, particularly among Muslim factions, as fighting escalated among various segments of Lebanon's fractious population. This section includes a reference to the bombing of the U.S. Embassy in Beirut on 18 April 1983, an attack—reportedly carried out by the terrorist group known as the Islamic Jihad—that killed 61 people including 17 Americans.

Noted in this section is the fact that there was no change to the mission of the Marines during this period, and no fundamental shift in the MAU's composition or defensive posture, even though the events that constituted a shift in the operational environment from benign to hostile—such as the Embassy bombing in April—were well known to the various MAU commanders. The section subtitled "Security of the Battalion Landing Team Headquarters" reviews the security conditions that prevailed in the MAU headquarters compound located at the Beirut International Airport. This section includes a reference to the Rules of Engagement (ROE) that the MAU commander defined for the Marines under his command.

The case ends with a brief description of the actual attack, which occurred early on the morning of 23 October 1983.

Where to Use the Case

The Bombing of the Marine Barracks is a powerful case and has proved effective at two distinct levels of military education.

For junior personnel, especially those involved in counterintelligence duties or as intelligence advisers to a commander, the case provides a stark lesson of what can happen when the fundamentals of force protection are overlooked. Courses at the Navy and Marine Corps Intelligence Training Center, for example, or in the Marine Counterintelligence Teams are ideal venues for this use of the case study.

For more senior personnel, especially officers destined for command at the battalion level or higher, or in staff positions at Unified Commands, the case highlights the need for consistency between a force's defensive posture—including its ROE—and its operational environment. Students at this level are more likely to be encountered at the Naval War College, the Marine Corps Command and Staff College, or at the JMIC.

Sources

The chief sources for this case included an unpublished doctoral dissertation by Dr. Jack Matthews, a retired Marine lieutenant colonel who served in one of the MAUs assigned to Beirut; the report of the Long Commission, noted in the case study; and interviews with Marines—chiefly counterintelligence personnel—who were directly involved in the events described. The JFK School of Government case study entitled "The U.S. Marines in Lebanon," added little to understanding of the event, possibly because its author did not have access to direct participants. Col. Timothy Geraghty, USMC (Ret.), the commander of the MAU that suffered the attack, reviewed the case in detail but was not a source in its creation.

Teaching Objectives

There are four teaching objectives for a discussion of this case. Instructors may shift their emphasis on these, depending on the level of instruction at which the case study is used.

At junior levels, students who discuss this case study should learn that:

Intelligence officers have an obligation to inform the commander clearly and forcefully on changes in the operational environment that require a shift in the defensive posture of the force.

Intelligence officers have an obligation to develop a detailed understanding of the social and political environments in which a military force operates, and to inform the commander on the probable sociopolitical impact of the force's behavior on the attitudes of the local population; this is particularly important in military operations other than war.

At a more senior level, students should reflect on two concepts in a discussion of this case study:

The commander has an obligation to assure reasonable consistency between a force's mission and its operational environment; when these become inconsistent, the commander should ask for clarification or modification to the mission.

The commander has a responsibility to direct a defensive posture for a force that is consistent with the operational environment. If higher headquarters is reluctant to provide the resources that the commander decides are necessary, he has an obligation to insist that the resources be made available. Like all command responsibilities, this cannot be delegated.

A Teaching Plan

Military personnel at all levels are characteristically mission-oriented, so to begin a discussion of this case study one may ask, "What was the mission of this force?" This question quickly reveals the sharp distinction between the mission of the first MAU— charged with an orderly evacuation of the PLO and certain elements of the Syrian Army—with the second mission, quoted in the section "The Plan Unravels." Students are likely to observe that the first was limited and clear, while the second was both ambitious and hazy. "What led to the expression of the second mission?" instructors might ask. Students will observe that the second or "nation-building" mission was expressed immediately following the Christian Phalange slaughter of the Palestinian refugees, with Palestinian and international outrage aggravated by U.S. Ambassador Philip Habib's commitment to the PLO leadership to prevent precisely the sort of atrocity that occurred. (Many students find it hard to believe that Habib did not inform the Marine commanders of this commitment; nevertheless, this is true.) A general understanding of the second mission and its distinction from the first should take about 10 minutes to define.

As a second question, an instructor may ask, "How would you describe the tactical environment that prevailed when the MAU arrived in late September 1982 to take on this mission?" As students address this question, they may be pressed for evidence to support their evaluations. In discussing the environment when the force arrived, students typically disagree, with some observing that it was benign and others that it merely appeared benign, when in fact it was not. If students insist that the environment was deceptively benign, the question may be shifted to focus on the Marines' early operations and defensive measures; these suggest that whatever the true nature of the operational environment, the various MAU commanders apparently believed that their force was perceived as neutral and generally welcome. A discussion of the tactical environment at the beginning of the intervention should take about 10 minutes.

At this point, students can describe how the environment changed over the course of the next 13 months, with evidence of the changes they describe. This part of the discussion will reveal increasingly obvious signs of hostility during early 1983. These included the shift in "atmospherics" reported by Captain Johnson, the increased level of active fighting among Lebanese factions, attacks on Marine patrols in February and March, and the bombing of the U.S. Embassy in April. A general understanding of the shift in the tactical environment should require about 10 minutes to develop.

An appropriate question at this point is "How did the behavior of the MAU affect the attitudes of the local population?" This question will reveal how the Marines' preference for socializing exclusively with Christians (who were more likely to speak English than the Muslim groups in Beirut) created an impression that the Marines were not truly neutral. For example, the social gathering featuring as guest of honor the leader of the Christian Phalange—the group that had carried out the gruesome massacre at the refugee camps only eight weeks earlier—appears in retrospect to be a gross miscalculation. Instructors should be able to return to this topic during their summary to reinforce the teaching objective concerning the responsibilities of intelligence personnel as advisers to a commander. A discussion of this question should require about five minutes.

When using this case for mid-level officers destined for command or senior staff positions, instructors during this part of the discussion may wish to use a question to draw students' attention to the reaction of higher headquarters—in this case the European Command (EUCOM) in Stuttgart—to the emerging evidence that signaled a shift from benign to hostile. As noted in the case, a EUCOM officer described the Embassy bombing as "a peripheral event not reflecting local or popular opposition [and] not related to the basic mission of peacekeeping." Students typically express shock at this reaction to an event as violent and destructive as the Embassy bombing, and instructors may use this to point out the gap between the actual tactical environment and EUCOM's understanding of the situation. Instructors may wish to explore the implications of this gap for a commander concerned about the safety of his forces. This exploration should require about five minutes.

Shifting to the next block of analysis, students should ponder "What did the MAU do in response to the emerging evidence that the tactical environment had changed?" Other than a change in the Rules of Engagement at the British Embassy, the Durafour Building, and the Ambassador's residence, the answer is, "Nothing."

"What were the options open to the MAU commander?" is a useful probing question, as at this point the class may explore what Col. Geraghty could have done differently. Students typically observe that there were numerous ways in which the MAU commander could have improved his force protection posture. Some of these (such as dispersing the force by shifting some of the troops back aboard the ships, where they would have been relatively safe) would not have required permission from higher headquarters. Others, such as moving the MAU out of the airport entirely, erecting solid barriers around the barracks, or changing the ROE would have required permission or at least extensive coordination. This part of the discussion should require about 10 minutes.

At this point, instructors may wish to draw students' attention to exhibit 2, a map of the barracks compound, and ask, "Against what types of threat is this defense designed?" Students typically observe that the defensive posture of the MAU revealed an awareness of conventional threats such as mortars and sniper fire, but was ineffective against a vehicular bomb. Exhibit 2 suggests that the MAU commander—and his force protection advisers—either could not conceive of the threat that in the end destroyed the MAU and led to the U.S. decision to end the intervention or they did not take defensive measures consistent with their understanding.

If students observe that the commander and his staff simply could not imagine the possibility of a suicide bomber in a vehicle, one may ask, "Why not?" The embassy had been destroyed only six months previously, and even though the vehicle in that incident was parked and not moving, it certainly should have been obvious that terrorist groups operating in Lebanon had the capability to create and use large bombs loaded in cars or trucks. Moreover, on the last page of the case, corroborative reports from Marine sentries indicate that the guards on duty immediately concluded that the vehicle represented a hostile attack; if they could reach that conclusion so quickly, why was the possibility outside the range of the commander's vision, and that of his staff?

This part of the discussion represents the heart of the objectives, and should be fully explored, requiring about 15 minutes.

As a final exercise, students should consider how responsibility for the outcome should be assigned. (This question may not be necessary for relatively junior groups, in which case it can be disregarded.) Most students probably will conclude that Col. Geraghty is primarily responsible, but that he shares this responsibility with his senior staff and with higher headquarters; both levels failed in their obligation to provide him timely, relevant intelligence and command guidance. After about 10 minutes of discussion of this question, instructors may distribute the (B) case, which is a short excerpt from the report of the Long Commission. I suggest leaving a few minutes for a summary, during which instructors may use what they have put up on the board to reinforce the basic objectives of the discussion.

ABOUT THE AUTHOR

Tom Shreeve is the creator of the Community's Case Method Program and was its director for several years. He learned the craft of case method teaching first as an MBA student at Harvard Business School from 1981 to 1983, and later as a research associate and casewriter. Tom has taught throughout the Intelligence Community using cases, and is the author of about one-third of the current catalog of cases and case studies. Tom was a Marine Corps Reserve officer, a member of the Master's Program for Reserves faculty of the Joint Military Intelligence College, and of the Adjunct Faculty at the Marine Corps Command and Staff College in Quantico, Virginia. He maintains a website on the Intelligence Community Case Method Program at *http://www.intelcasestudies.com* and he may be contacted at *tomshreeve@aol.com.*